SUPER SIMPLE QUILTS #1
AMISH DIAMOND

KATHLEEN EATON

CONTEMPORARY
QUILTING

Chilton Book Company
Radnor, Pennsylvania

To Joe, Joan, Rose and Chuck
Thank you for your loving support and encouragement.

ACKNOWLEDGMENTS

I'm grateful for the photographic talents of Michael Boburka, who assisted with black-and-white photography, and the artistic talents of Katharine Schwengel, who assisted with line drawings. Special thanks to them and to the many other people who made this book possible, especially Mom and Dad, Barb and Jim, Robbie Fanning, Tim Scott, Nancy Zieman, Jessica, Charlie, David, Tom, Sue, and the people of the Camera Fair in Marinette, Wisconsin.

INTRODUCTION

This pattern is a true Amish quilt pattern from the nineteenth century. The Amish people lived a very bland life, without much color or variety, but used vibrant color in their quilted creations. The Amish Diamond pattern is as contemporary today as it was 100 years ago. Although you would rarely find a print fabric in an authentic Amish-made quilt, that doesn't mean you can't use prints in yours!

Whether you are an expert quilter or just beginning to discover the joy and satisfaction of quiltmaking, this pattern was made for you. Now you can custom-make a handcrafted quilt, in sizes from twin to king, that will last for years, at a fraction of the cost of a store-bought comforter, in a fraction of the time you thought it would take. In fact, this pattern was designed to be completed in less than two days! And you can take pride in knowing you did it yourself.

Included with this quilt project are instructions for accessory items—a crib quilt, wall hanging, throw pillow, pillow sham, chair pad, and placemat. Use your imagination and decorate every room in your home!

The secret of successful quilting is . . . *Keep it super simple!*

Designed by Anthony Jacobson
Cover photo by Tim Scott taken at James Lewis Development, Charlestown, Pa.
Manufactured in the United States of America

Library of Congress Catalog Card Number 92-53149
ISBN 0-8019-8335-5

1 2 3 4 5 6 7 8 9 0   1 0 9 8 7 6 5 4 3 2

Make a Quilt

In this section you will find all the information you need to make a twin, full, queen, or king-size quilt. Instructions for making a crib-size quilt or wall hanging begin on page 1-9.

Getting Started

This pattern actually comes from an early Amish quilt. Traditional Amish colors of dark grape, hunter green, royal blue, and black make a very pleasing combination and will give your quilt lasting appeal.

You will get the best results by using four bold, strongly contrasting colors to give optimum emphasis to the pattern. Bright red, blue, yellow, and green are a great combination, as well as softer, more pastel tones of these same colors. And teens will love a combination of white, gray, black, and red.

Materials Needed

Fabric

Yardage amounts listed below are approximate and will allow for some leftover fabric—enough to make several pillows or two pillow shams or a wall hanging or baby quilt. Yardages for backing are given in the next section.

Batting and Backing

Polyester fiberfill or wool or cotton batting large enough to complete your quilt.

A large, flat sheet or extra-wide fabric, large enough to use as a backing on your quilt. Three yards of 108″ sheeting (available at well-supplied fabric stores) will fit all sizes. Or you can use 44/45″ wide fabric as follows: *For twin and full sizes,* you need 5½ yards of 44/45″ wide fabric, cut into two pieces, each 2¾ yards long. Seam them together along the selvage (Fig. 1-1) *For queen and king sizes,* you need 8¼ yards of 44/45″ wide fabric, cut in three pieces, each 2¾ yards long, seamed together along the selvages (Fig. 1-2).

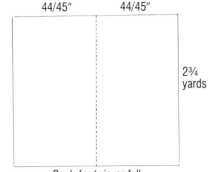

Fig. 1-1   Back for twin or full

Fig. 1-2   Back for queen or king

When laying out the backing, batting, and quilt top, center the quilt top so the seams in the back are equal distances from the sides.

Don't Forget

Thread (for piecing your quilt face, as well as for hand or machine quilting, if desired)

String, yarn, or 1/16″ ribbon for tying your quilt, if you prefer

Graph paper or plain paper (which you have scored with 1″ squares) for pattern making

Making the Pattern

Making the pattern is as easy as counting squares and connecting dots. The pattern guides

	Fabric 1	Fabric 2	Fabric 3	Fabric 4
Twin (90″ × 68″)	2¾ yds.	2½ yds.	1½ yds.	1⅝ yds.
Full (90″ × 76″)	2¾ yds.	2½ yds.	1½ yds.	1⅝ yds.
Queen (90″ × 90″)	2¾ yds.	2½ yds.	1½ yds.	1⅝ yds.
King (90″ × 102″)	4⅓ yds.	3¼ yds.	1½ yds.	1⅝ yds.

on pages 1-15 and 1-16 give dimensions for making your own pattern pieces for your project. You may use graph paper, gridded freezer paper, or tracing paper taped to a 1″ gridded cutting board. Graph paper is available in a variety of "squares-to-the-inch" sizes. It doesn't matter what size you choose, as long as the 1″ lines are clearly visible. If you are using smaller pieces of graph paper, carefully tape them together using clear tape, making sure the lines match up vertically and horizontally.

Start by marking a dot on the corner of one square on the grid. This represents one corner of your pattern. Using the 1″ grid on your paper, count, either straight up or down or sideways, exactly the number of inches (squares) indicated on the pattern guides on pages 1-15 and 1-16. It helps to have an extra ruler on hand to add a fraction of an inch where needed. Mark another dot when you have reached the number of squares you want, and draw a line between the dots. Continue in this manner until the pattern piece is complete.

Before drawing your angled lines, first draw the straight horizontal and vertical lines. Then just connect the ends of these lines to create the angled line to complete your pattern piece.

Do not add seam allowances! Unlike in some quilt pattern books, these patterns already include a ⅜″ seam allowance.

After you have drawn pattern pieces A through G on the grid, double-check all measurements, and carefully cut them out (Fig. 1-3).

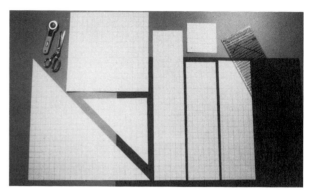

Fig. 1-3

Cutting the Fabric

Rotary cutting tools are ideal for cutting your strips and pattern pieces. Before cutting the patchwork pattern pieces, cut the side strips as follows:

Bed size	Fabric 1	Fabric 2
Twin	2 each, 11″ × 66″ 2 each, 5″ × 98″	2 each, 11″ × 56″ 2 each, 5″ × 78″
Full	2 each, 11″ × 76″ 2 each, 8″ × 98″	2 each, 11″ × 56″ 2 each, 8″ × 78″
Queen	2 each, 11″ × 78″ 2 each, 10″ × 98″	2 each, 11″ × 56″ 2 each, 10″ × 78″
King	2 each, 11″ × 84″ 2 each, 14″ × 98″	2 each, 11″ × 56″ 2 each, 14″ × 78″

Note: The center pattern of the quilt is the same for all four bed sizes. The variation in quilt size comes from the different sizes used in the side strips, which are added after the quilt center is pieced. The strip sizes shown above are generous, to allow for slight variations in seam allowances or stretch the fabric. You may trim away the excess after the strip is sewn in place.

After you have cut the long strips of fabric, cut the remaining pattern pieces. The number of pieces needed are shown on the pattern guides on pages 1-15 and 1-16.

Sewing the Main Quilt Block

Hint #1: When one or both pattern pieces are being sewn on a bias or angle-cut edge, it helps to pin the edges together to prevent pulling or stretching the fabric. Otherwise, it is not necessary to pin pieces together before sewing them. In fact, it's quicker and easier not to. Just be sure you're letting the machine do the work, and that you're not pulling, or "force-guiding," the fabric, which causes bias-cut fabrics to stretch or distort. You can also eliminate this potential problem by using a walking foot on your sewing machine.

Hint #2: Don't worry if your edges don't match perfectly when you are sewing them together. The seams are hidden inside the quilt. And the quilting stitches or ties help camouflage minor flaws. It's the total finished look that will make you proud to give or display your handiwork.

Hint #3: As you work, press all seam allowances toward the darker of the fabrics. This prevents seam allowances from being noticeable through lighter-colored fabrics.

1. After cutting out all the pieces, lay them on a flat surface (Fig. 1-4). Working from the center square, sew the pieces together using a ³⁄₈″ seam allowance, as follows.

Fig. 1-5

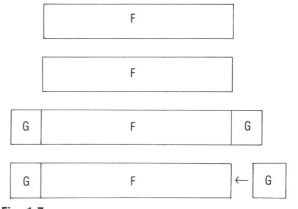

Fig. 1-6

4. Sew squares G to opposite ends of *two* F strips (Fig. 1-7).

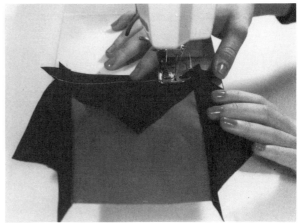

Fig. 1-7

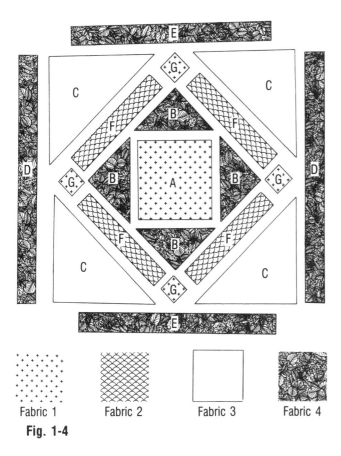

Fig. 1-4

2. Sew small triangle B to square A, centering the square so the points of the triangle are wider than the square (Fig. 1-5).

3. Sew another small triangle B to the opposite side of the square. Then sew the two remaining B triangles to the remaining sides of the square (Fig. 1-6).

5. Sew two F strips (without the G squares sewn on) to opposite sides of the center square (Fig. 1-8). Next sew the remaining F strips, with the G squares sewn to opposite ends, to the remaining sides, aligning the seams to create matched corners. This completes a new center square.

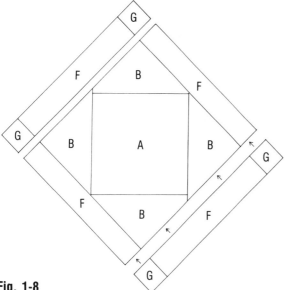

Fig. 1-8

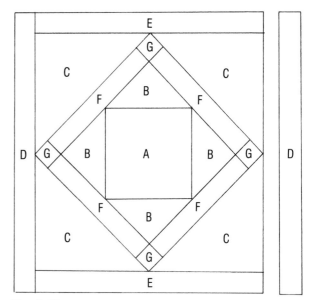

Fig. 1-10

6. Sew large triangles C to center square, as in Steps 2 and 3, complete a new center square (Fig. 1-9).

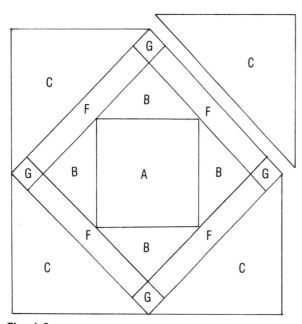

Fig. 1-9

7. Sew strips E to opposite sides of the center square. Sew strips D to the remaining sides (Fig. 1-10). You may need to trim a slight excess from these strips as they are sewn into place. Your main quilt block is now complete.

Sewing on the Side Strips

1. Sew the shorter strips of Fabric 2 to the top and bottom of your finished quilt center. (See Fig. 1-11.) Trim any excess.

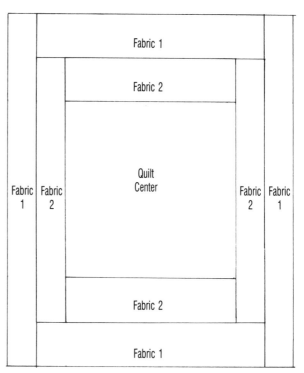

Fig. 1-11

2. Sew the longer strips of Fabric 2 to the two opposite edges, including in the seam the strips that were already added (creating a large rectangle).

3. Next, sew the shorter strips of Fabric 1 to the same sides the first strips were sewn to.

4. Finally, sew the remaining (longest) strips of Fabric 1 to the last two sides of the quilt to complete the face. Press all seams toward dark.

Finishing the Quilt

1. Cut and seam the backing fabric, if necessary, to equal the size of your finished quilt top. (See directions on page 1-3.)

2. Lay the backing (sheet, sheeting, or seamed fabric) right side down on a large, clean surface.

3. Place the polyester fiberfill or other batting on top of the backing.

4. Lay the quilt top, right side up, on the fiberfill. Hand baste, or pin, using large safety pins, through all layers to hold them in place. (I prefer safety pins to straight pins because they save my hands and other body parts from pinpricks as I work.)

5. Using yarn, string, or $\frac{1}{16}''$ ribbon, tie the layers firmly at the points shown on Fig. 1-14. Or quilt the layers by hand or machine, as desired. Instructions follow.

6. Finish the edges, using bias tape (Fig. 1-12) or other decorative trim, as desired. The edges can also be turned easily to the inside and sewn in place by machine (Fig. 1-13). You can insert piping, lace, or a ruffle at the edge with this method.

There are many ways to apply a bias taped edge, but in general, it is easiest if you sew a seam around your entire project, using a narrow seam allowance, to keep the layers from stretching or shifting *before* you apply the bias tape.

Starting in the middle of one side of your project, and using long straight pins, pin the bias tape around the entire piece, overlapping and folding under the last edge where it meets with your starting point. When you get to a corner, tuck the excess flatly and neatly inside of itself, by gently pushing it to one side with pointed scissors or a pin. It may help to open the bias tape so it is flat when you get to a corner, then pinch the excess to guide it into the fold at the corner. Hand baste or topstitch by machine over the miter.

There are a number of quilt books available with chapters devoted to finishing the edges of your quilt. Some books have been written solely on the subject. Your local library or bookstore should have a variety of books to choose from.

To Tie Your Quilt

Tying your quilt is the easiest method of holding the layers together and provides a quick finish to your quilt. I suggest basting or pinning the layers of your quilt to hold them in place before starting to tie. It is not necessary to mark the points at which you will tie your quilt. Figure 1-14 shows where the ties should be placed.

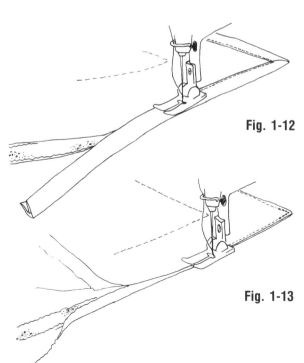

Fig. 1-12

Fig. 1-13

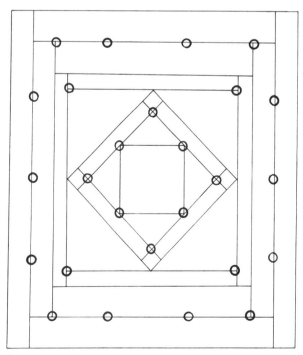

Fig. 1-14

Thread a large needle (one with a large eye, such as a tapestry needle) with yarn, 1/16" ribbon, or string (button or quilting thread also works well). Working from the top of the quilt, push the needle through all layers, drawing the thread through, but not all the way. Leave a 6"–8" tail sticking out on top. About 1/8–1/4" from the first stitch, draw the needle back up (from the back to the front) through all layers. Cut the thread, again leaving a tail about 6"–8" long. Tie these two tails tightly together, using a double or triple knot to hold the tie securely in place.

You can make a bow with the excess, or simply trim the tails to about 1".

To Quilt by Machine

After the layers are securely pinned or basted, roll up one-half of the quilt tightly enough to allow it to fit under the head of your sewing machine. You can safety-pin it closed or use bicycle clips to hold the roll. With larger quilts, you may need a friend to help guide the bulk through while you are quilting the center block.

Start by quilting the center area as Fig. 1-15 shows, to anchor and secure the layers. After you have stitched the quilting lines shown in Fig. 1-15, continue quilting around the center square, leaving the needle in the down position at the corners. As you go, carefully turn and reposition the quilt so the layers don't shift. It also helps to smooth the top and bottom toward you occasionally, with one hand above and one hand below, palms pressed gently together, and fingers spread.

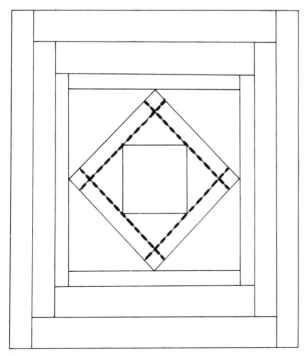

Fig. 1-15

Continue quilting by machine, following the outline of the pattern by sewing along all the seam lines of the pieced quilt top. Be sure to back-tack the beginning and ending of each quilting seam. I like to use thread that matches one of the lighter fabrics. When quilting along a seam that joins a solid color to a print fabric, try to keep your quilting stitches on the printed fabric, just to the side of the seam.

Today's polyester fiberfills don't clump or shift as much as natural battings made of wool or cotton, because of the resins that hold the polyester fibers together. The stitching lines suggested here are adequate to hold polyester fiberfill in place, but you may wish to add some extra quilting lines or ties if using pure wool or cotton batting.

Alternate Method of Finishing

1. Another method of finishing your quilt is to sew the face to the backing, right sides together, leaving the top edge open. Because these seams are so long, it helps to pin the edges together before sewing, to hold them in place. Be sure the back is cut to the exact size of the face before sewing them together.

2. Before turning right side out, lay your top and backing, which have been sewn together on three sides, right side down on a large, clean, flat surface. If you don't have a large enough floor space, lay it on as large a table as you can, with the open, unseamed end hanging over the edge of the table, and the bottom half of the quilt lying flat on the table. Place the polyester fiberfill on top and trim it to the exact size of the quilt.

3. Starting at the end opposite the opening, roll the entire quilt, like a sleeping bag, or jelly roll, until you have a long "tube" of fabric and batting (Fig. 1-16).

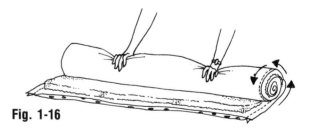

Fig. 1-16

4. Carefully reach inside the layers of fabric (between the face and backing), and slowly pull the tube inside-out, through the opening (Fig. 1-17).

Fig. 1-17

5. Slowly unwrap the quilt (Fig. 1-18), which will open, filled with fiberfill, and with three of the edges finished. (Practice with a sock. First, roll the sock, starting at the toe, and pull the cuff back over the roll. Slowly unroll it from the inside out, reaching inside the sock, between the layers, and pulling gently on the roll.)

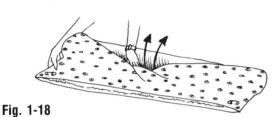
Fig. 1-18

6. Lay the quilt on a large, flat surface, and pin or baste through all layers. Hand or machine quilt, or tie it, as described above.

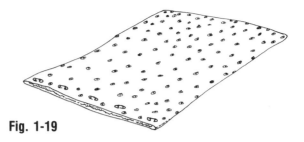
Fig. 1-19

7. Turn the remaining edges to the inside, pin to hold (Fig. 1-19), and machine stitch to close.

Make a Crib Quilt (42″ × 52″)

Materials Needed

Fabric

Fabric 1, 1¾ yards
Fabric 2, ⅓ yard
Fabric 3 and 4, ½ yard each

Batting and Backing

Polyester fiberfill: 44″ × 54″
Backing fabric: 1¾ yards of 44/45″ wide fabric

Don't Forget

Thread (for piecing your quilt face, as well as for hand or machine quilting, if desired)
String, yarn, or 1/16″ ribbon for tying your quilt, if you prefer
Graph paper or plain paper (which you have scored with 1″ squares) for pattern making

1. Make your pattern pieces A through G in the dimensions given on the pattern guides on pages 1-15 and 1-16. Refer to "Getting Started" and "Making the Pattern" in the instructions for the large quilts. (This pattern is simply a miniature version of the main quilt block of the large quilt, minus one of the side strips.)

2. Before cutting pieces A through G out of your fabric, cut the side strips out of Fabric 1: two pieces 8″ × 39″ and two pieces 4″ × 54″.

3. Now cut out fabric pieces A through G.

4. Refer to "Sewing the Main Quilt Block," "Sewing on the Side Strips," and "Finishing the Quilt" in the instructions for the large quilts to complete the crib quilt. (You will be adding only one set of side strips.) The "Alternate Method of Finishing" (p. 1-8) is particularly nice when used on the crib quilt project.

Make a Wall Hanging (36″ square)

Materials Needed

Fabric

Fabric 1, ⅓ yard
Fabric 2, ⅓ yard

Fabrics 3 and 4, ½ yard each

Batting and Backing

Polyester fiberfill: 38″ square
Backing fabric: 1¼ yards, cut to fit face of wall hanging

Don't Forget

Thread (for piecing your quilt face, as well as for hand or machine quilting, if desired)

String, yarn, or 1/16″ ribbon for tying your quilt, if you prefer

Graph paper or plain paper (which you have scored with 1″ squares) for pattern making

1. Make your pattern pieces A through G in the dimensions given on the pattern guides on pages 1-15 and 1-16. Refer to "Getting Started" and "Making the Pattern" in the instructions for the large quilts. (This pattern is simply a miniature version of the main quilt block of the large quilt; no additional side strips are used for the wall hanging.)

2. Cut out all fabric pieces.

3. Refer to "Sewing the Main Quilt Block" and "Finishing the Quilt" in the instructions for the large quilts to complete the wall hanging. (The wall hanging has no added side strips.) The "Alternate Method of Finishing" (p. 1-8) is particularly nice when used on the wall hanging project.

You will probably want to make loops of fabric to sew to the top of the wall hanging or just behind the upper edge (hidden) to allow for a dowel rod to hang it.

To Make the Loops

For **hidden loops**, cut three pieces of fabric 1½″ × 4″. Fold the long edges inward to meet at the center, then fold the whole strip in half lengthwise. Using a straight stitch, sew through all layers along the "open" edge to make a small "ribbon" of fabric. Attach one in the middle of the upper edge of the wall hanging, and the remaining two at either side on the upper edge. Tack these to the

wall hanging through all layers using your sewing machine, or hand sew them in place.

For **decorative loops** (Fig. 1-20), cut three pieces of matching fabric 3″ × 5″. Fold these in half, right sides together, to create 1½″ × 5″ pieces. Using a 3/8″ seam allowance, sew a straight line down the 5″ raw edge. Turn these tubes right side out and press so the seam is centered on one side. Fold these in half widthwise to hide the seam. Attach to the top of your wall hanging by machine, spacing the loops evenly.

For **bow loops**, cut three pieces of wide ribbon, each 24″ long. Fold these in half and tack them to the top edge of your wall hanging by hand or machine, evenly spaced. Tie these loosely around a decorative pole or dowel rod.

The wall hanging is a perfect size for use as a table topper, lap quilt, or sofa throw.

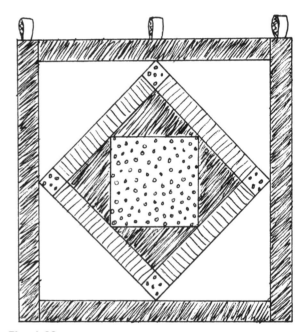

Fig. 1-20

Make a 16″ Throw Pillow

Fabric Requirements

Face: Use leftover scrap from large quilt or 1/8 yard of each of the four fabrics

Back: ½ yard of a matching fabric or a coordinating solid

Ruffle or cord: 5/8 yard of a matching fabric to make your own matching ruffle or bias cording. Or purchase 2 yards of prepackaged bias cording or ruffle.

1. Make pillow pattern pieces A through G in the dimensions given in the pattern guides on pages 1-15 and 1-16. See "Getting Started" and "Making the Pattern" in the instructions for the large quilt. Cut all fabric pieces.

2. Starting with the center square, and using a 3/8″ seam allowance, sew all pieces to complete the block according to Figs. 1-4 through 1-10. Press all seams toward darker fabrics.

3. You may quilt the pillow face before constructing the pillow. If so, layer it with a backing and fiberfill, cut to the same size as the face, then hand or machine quilt along the seams. It is not necessary to quilt the pillow; this is a matter of preference.

4. See the instructions for making ruffling and bias cording, page 1-12 With raw edges together, sew bias cording or a ruffle around the entire pillow face with a ⅜″ seam allowance. The raw edges of the cording match the raw edges of the pillow face (Fig. 1-21). You will need about 2 yards of bias cording or finished ruffling to go around the pillow. For a knife-edge pillow, with no extra trim, you can eliminate this step.

Fig. 1-21

5. Cut two pieces of backing fabric, 10″ × 17″. Finish one 17″ edge on each of these two pieces with a double-folded ¼″ hem, machine stitched.

6. Lay the pillow right side up, with ruffle or cording toward the center. Place the backing right side down on the pillow, overlapping the finished edges evenly in the center. Pin around the edges (Fig. 1-22).

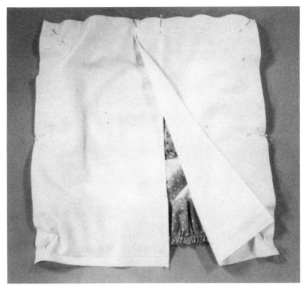

Fig. 1-22

7. Sew around the entire pillow, following the seam used to sew the cording or ruffle in place, or using a ⅜″ seam allowance. Turn inside out through the overlapped backing. Trim away any excess around the seams before turning.

8. Insert a 15″ or 16″ pillow form.

Make Your Own 15″–16″ Pillow Form

1. Save your scrap fiberfill.

2. Cut two 18″ squares of any white or ivory fabric.

3. Sew these together on three sides, using a ½″ seam allowance. Turn right side out.

4. Cut two 17″ squares of leftover fiberfill, and carefully slide them into the pillow cover. Continue to stuff smaller bits of fiberfill between the squares, until the pillow is plump, but not too hard.

5. To finish, whipstitch the opening by hand. I call this a 15″–16″ finished size because the finished size will vary according to the plumpness of the pillow.

Make a Removable Chair Pad Cover

Note: An additional ⅓ yard of one of the fabrics is required for each chair pad.

1. Complete the 16″ pillow cover as explained above in "Make a 16″ Throw Pillow."

2. Cut two strips of fabric, 44″ × 5″. With a roll-hem attachment for your sewing machine, or a narrow double fold, hem around all sides of both strips. Fold each in half, matching the two short ends to create two tie ends, and pinch or pleat at the fold to gather. At what will be the back two corners, machine stitch the ties to the pillow cover, on the underside of the finished pillow, under the ruffle (Fig. 1-23).

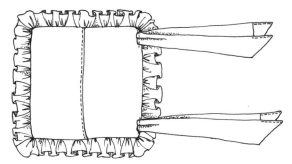

Fig. 1-23

3. To make a removable chair pad insert, purchase or make a 15″–16″ pillow form. With a long needle and double heavy-duty thread, run the thread through the center of the pillow form, leaving a "tail" of thread about 6″ long. Bring the needle back through about ½″ from the first stitch, and tie the ends of the thread, pulling tightly to form a "tuft" in the center.

Two matching chair pads make a lovely rocker set. (Fig. 1-24).

Fig. 1-24

How to Make Matching Ruffling and Bias Cording for Pillows, Shams, and Chair Pads

Ruffling

You will need about ⅝″ yard of extra fabric for ruffles around pillows and chair pads. You will need about ⅞ yard for pillow shams.

1. From the width of the fabric (44/45″) cut three 7″ strips (four strips for pillow shams), and sew them together on the short ends to make a long circle of fabric. Press the seam allowances open.

2. Fold the circle in half lengthwise so the raw edges meet and right sides face out. Press.

3. With a wide basting stitch, sew about ¼″ from the raw edge (Fig. 1-25).

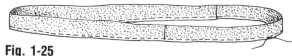

Fig. 1-25

4. Divide the circle equally into quarters, identifying the quarter marks with a straight pin. Pin the circle to the center of each straight edge on all four sides of your project, using the pins that mark the quarters to hold the ruffle in place.

5. Pull the basting stitch until the circle gathers evenly into a ruffle equal to the size of the project that you are working on. Use straight pins to hold the ruffle in place around the outer edge of the project as you gather it to fit (Fig. 1-26).

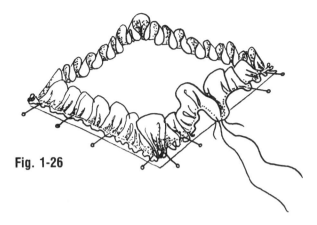

Fig. 1-26

Bias Cording

You will need ⅝ yard of matching fabric to make your own bias cording.

1. Cut 1½"-wide strips of fabric on the bias of the fabric. The strip of bias-cut fabric should be several inches longer than the measurement around the edge of the project you wish to trim. You may have to seam your pieces to arrive at the proper length.

2. Using purchased cording, wrap the bias strip around the cording so that wrong sides and raw edges meet. Using a zipper foot, stitch close to the cord, but not too snug, through both layers of fabric (Fig. 1-27).

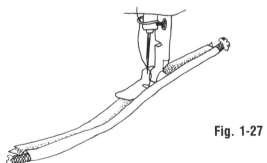

Fig. 1-27

3. The simplest application of the finished bias tape is to begin sewing it on one straight edge in the center of that side, keeping the raw edges of the bias tape and your project even, but with the starting end angled off the edge. Sew around the entire project, clipping the seam allowance of the bias tape at the corners. When you reach your starting point, overlap the bias tape, sewing over the angled end, and carefully angle the final end to sew it off the edge (Fig. 1-28). Clip it to trim.

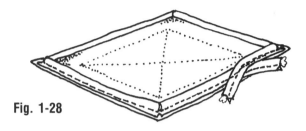

Fig. 1-28

You may also apply bias tape by starting in the middle of one side, but start your seam about 2" from the end of the bias tape. Sew all around as described above, but when you get to where you started, open the seam on the 2" tail of the bias tape and pull back the fabric to show the cord. Clip off the 2" of cord, and fold the fabric that is left in half, to create a 1" tail (fold the fabric to the inside, so that only the face side shows). Cut the other end of the bias tape so it ends exactly where the first cord now starts. Wrap the folded bias tape fabric around this raw edge, and finish your seam.

Make a Placemat

Fabric Requirements

Face: Use leftover scrap from quilt or ⅛ yard of each of the four fabrics

Back: ½ yard of fabric will allow enough for two placemats

1. Make your pattern pieces A through G in the dimensions given on the pattern guides on pages 1-15 and 1-16. See "Getting Started" and "Making the Pattern" in the instructions for the large quilts. Cut out all fabric pieces.

2. Starting with the center square, and using a ⅜" seam allowance, sew all pieces to complete the block according to Figs. 1-4 through 1-10. Press all seams toward darker fabric.

3. Cut two strips of fabric, 2½" × 17", and sew them to opposite sides of the finished quilt block, trimming away any excess. Press all seams. This makes the placemat rectangular.

4. Cut a rectangle of backing fabric 17" × 20". Center this, right sides together, on the finished quilt block. Trim excess fabric from the quilt block to equal the size of the backing. Sew together with a ⅜" seam allowance all around, except for a 4" opening centered on one of the seams. Clip the corners and turn inside out through the opening. Hand or machine stitch the opening and press all around.

5. To minimize raveling or fraying of the seams on the inside when these are washed, you may wish to "quilt" along the seam lines, even though these do not have fiberfill. (You may add fiberfill, if you wish.)

Make a Standard Pillow Sham

Fabric Requirements

Face: Use leftover scrap from quilt, or ¼ yard of Fabrics 1 and 2 and ⅛ yard of Fabrics 3 and 4
Back: ⅔ yard
Ruffle: ⅞ yard

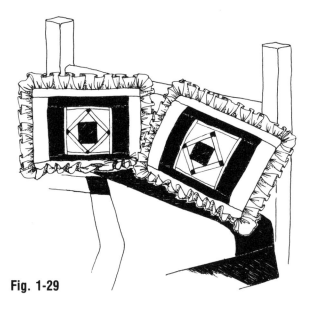

Fig. 1-29

1. Make your pattern pieces A through G in the dimensions given on the pattern guides on pages 1-15 and 1-16. See "Getting Started" and "Making the Pattern" in the instructions for the large quilts. Cut out all fabric pieces.

2. Starting with the center square and using a ⅜" seam allowance, sew all pieces to complete the block according to Figs. 1-4 through 1-10. Press all seams toward dark.

3. Cut two strips of Fabric 2, 3½" × 17", and two strips 2" × 23".

4. Cut two strips of Fabric 1, 3½" × 21", and two strips 2" × 29".

5. Add the 3½" × 17" strips of Fabric 2 to opposite sides of the quilt block, trimming away any excess. Add the 2" × 23" strips of the same fabric, in the same manner, to the remaining edges.

6. Add the 3½" × 21" strips of Fabric 1 to the first sides (as in Step 5), and add the remaining strips to the last two sides.

7. You may wish to first quilt the sham face by layering it with a backing and fiberfill cut to the same size as the face, then hand or machine quilt along the seams. This is not necessary. It's a matter of preference.

8. See the instructions for making ruffling and bias cording, page 1-12. With raw edges together, sew bias cording and/or a ruffle around the entire sham face with a ⅜" seam allowance. You will need about 3 yards of bias cording or finished ruffling to go around the pillow sham. (This is sewn to the face side of the pillow sham.)

9. Cut two pieces of a backing fabric, 16" × 24", finishing one 24" edge on each piece with a narrow double-folded ¼" hem, machine stitched.

10. Lay the pillow sham right side up, with ruffle pressed toward the center (Fig. 1-21). Place the backing, right side down, on the sham, overlapping the finished edges evenly in the center. Pin around the edges (see Fig. 1-22). Flip it over.

11. Sew around the entire pillow sham, following the seam used to sew the ruffling and/or cording in place. Turn inside out through the overlapped backing. Trim away any excess around the seams before turning right side out.

Amish Diamond Pattern Guides

Dimensions include ⅜″ seam allowance.

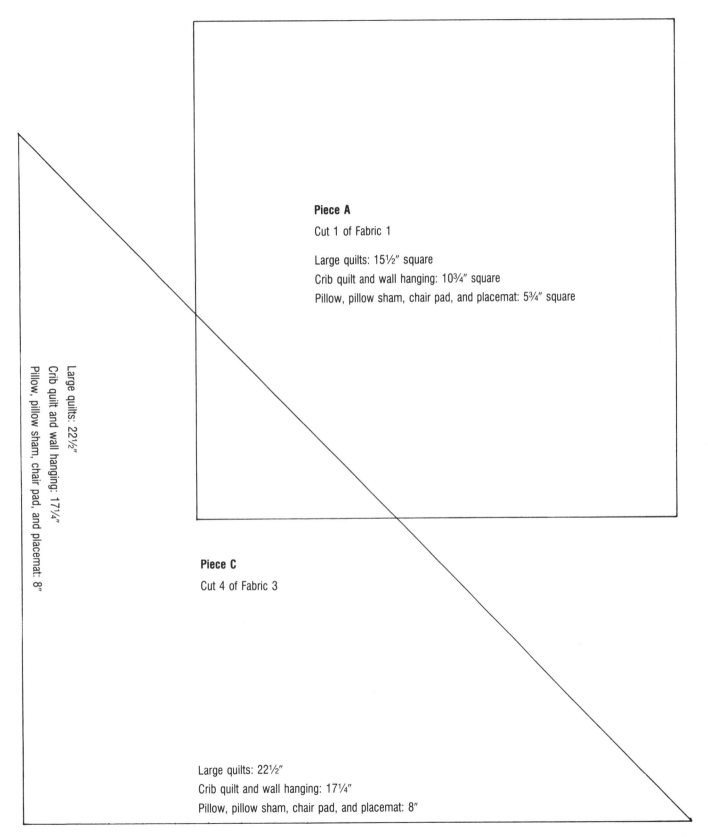

Piece A

Cut 1 of Fabric 1

Large quilts: 15½″ square
Crib quilt and wall hanging: 10¾″ square
Pillow, pillow sham, chair pad, and placemat: 5¾″ square

Large quilts: 22½″
Crib quilt and wall hanging: 17¼″
Pillow, pillow sham, chair pad, and placemat: 8″

Piece C

Cut 4 of Fabric 3

Large quilts: 22½″
Crib quilt and wall hanging: 17¼″
Pillow, pillow sham, chair pad, and placemat: 8″

Note: Instructions for making your templates in the correct dimensions can be found under ''Making the Pattern''.

Amish Diamond Pattern Guides

Dimensions include ⅜″ seam allowance.

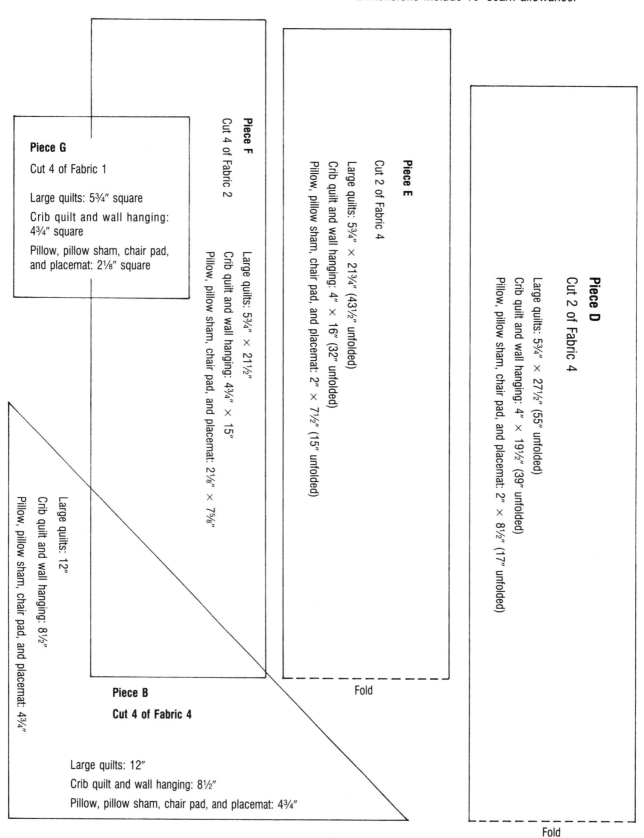

Piece G

Cut 4 of Fabric 1

Large quilts: 5¾″ square

Crib quilt and wall hanging: 4¾″ square

Pillow, pillow sham, chair pad, and placemat: 2⅛″ square

Piece F

Cut 4 of Fabric 2

Large quilts: 5¾″ × 21½″

Crib quilt and wall hanging: 4¾″ × 15″

Pillow, pillow sham, chair pad, and placemat: 2⅛″ × 7⅝″

Piece E

Cut 2 of Fabric 4

Large quilts: 5¾″ × 21¾″ (43½″ unfolded)

Crib quilt and wall hanging: 4″ × 16″ (32″ unfolded)

Pillow, pillow sham, chair pad, and placemat: 2″ × 7½″ (15″ unfolded)

Piece D

Cut 2 of Fabric 4

Large quilts: 5¾″ × 27½″ (55″ unfolded)

Crib quilt and wall hanging: 4″ × 19½″ (39″ unfolded)

Pillow, pillow sham, chair pad, and placemat: 2″ × 8½″ (17″ unfolded)

Fold

Piece B

Cut 4 of Fabric 4

Large quilts: 12″

Crib quilt and wall hanging: 8½″

Pillow, pillow sham, chair pad, and placemat: 4¾″

Large quilts: 12″

Crib quilt and wall hanging: 8½″

Pillow, pillow sham, chair pad, and placemat: 4¾″

Fold